THE OFFICIAL
HEART OF
MIDLOTHIAN
ANNUAL 2023

Written by Neil Hobson
Designed by Lucy Boyd

A Grange Publication

© 2022. Published by Grange Communications Ltd., Edinburgh, under licence from Heart of Midlothian. Printed in the EU.

Photographs © James Christie, David Mollison, Robert Doyle, SNS Group

ISBN 978-1-915295-48-4

CONTENTS

Hello, I'd like to give you a warm welcome to the Heart of Midlothian Football Club Annual 2023.

Thank you for picking up a copy of this year's annual. I hope within these pages, you can read and learn all about Hearts - and reflect on what was a very special season for the club. I know how memorable and enjoyable it was for the players, and for all of our supporters in the stands at Tynecastle.

We came into the new season with the aim of establishing ourselves as a Premiership team after securing promotion from the Championship. Hearts is a big club, and we felt like we could make a really big statement about what we're all about to the rest of the league now that we're back.

We were able to sign some really talented players; Cammy Devlin, Beni Baningime and Barrie McKay to name just a few! These guys weren't just tremendous footballers, but they also really bought into what we were trying to do at Hearts, and really understood what it is that makes this club so special to so many people. I was delighted that the club finished third, bringing European football back to Gorgie for the first time in many years.

On a personal note, I'm delighted to be going into next season as manager of this football club. I've been around Hearts for a long time now, both as a player and a coach. I still get the same buzz coming through the doors at Tynecastle that I had when I first joined as a young footballer back in 1996. A great deal has changed in that time, but one thing has remained constant - the incredible backing of you, the Hearts fans.

Walking out of the tunnel of the Main Stand on a match day, taking my seat in the dugout, and hearing the sounds of the Hearts Song along with the roar of the Gorgie crowd - there just isn't anything else quite like it. It's a job that none of us will ever take for granted.

Hearts, Hearts, Glorious Hearts!

Robbie Neilson
Manager

2021/22 SEASON REVIEW
Hearts are back!

As Hearts began preparations for our return to the Premiership after winning the Championship title to secure promotion, few down Gorgie way could have predicted what a remarkable season it turned out to be back in Scotland's premier division.

Robbie Neilson and Hearts' Sporting Director Joe Savage set about assembling a squad ready to show the Premiership that Hearts were back, and here to stay!

The club sadly bid farewell to players that helped win the title, whilst a clutch of new faces arrived as the boys in maroon set about getting back to the business of being a Premiership football club.

AUGUST

Hearts were back in the Premiership, and what a clash the fixture list threw up for the Jambos for the opening day of the season! Celtic came to Tynecastle for the first time under their new manager Ange Postecoglou. Widely tipped as the favourites, the Jambos stunned Celtic with a Gary Mackay-Steven goal and last-minute John Souttar header, clinching all three points for the men in maroon.

A thrilling victory, but one tinged with a sense of sadness with only 5,722 supporters allowed inside Tynecastle due to ongoing Covid restrictions.

Neilson's men followed up with a superb 2-1 victory over St. Mirren in Paisley; Andy Halliday scoring the first before Liam Boyce notched in the second half to get his first strike of the season! A trip to the north-east was next for Hearts, where they were forced to settle for a share of the spoils at Pittodrie against Aberdeen, with Funso Ojo scoring late on to cancel out a Liam Boyce strike.

An impressive first month was rounded off with a thrilling victory over Dundee United at Tannadice. Liam Boyce was on target yet again as the Jambos left Tayside with three points and a 2-0 win.

OCTOBER

Hearts kicked off October with a bang: defeating Motherwell 2-0 in Gorgie! Liam Boyce slotted home an early penalty before Stephen Kingsley curled in yet another free kick to ensure the Jambos maintained their unbeaten start.

A trip to Ibrox was next as the league leading JTs faced defending champions Rangers. John Lundstram netted on the cusp of half-time to set up a nervy second half for Hearts. The boys in maroon never gave up and were rewarded for their persistence when Craig Halkett scored in the 90th minute to earn Hearts a point in Govan.

October was rounded off with two more draws, with a clash against Dundee at Tynecastle finishing 1-1, and Josh Ginnelly salvaging a point for the Jambos in a 1-1 draw at McDiarmid Park.

The month ended with Hearts' first defeat of the season; Aberdeen winning 2-1 to take all three points at Pittodrie. Marley Watkins and Lewis Ferguson striking for the Dons.

SEPTEMBER

The month of September began with an Edinburgh derby at Tynecastle! Hearts last faced Hibs in October 2020 – with the Jambos sending Hibs packing at Hampden in the Scottish Cup semi-final. The match finished goalless, with bragging rights put on ice for another day. A draw with Ross County in Dingwall followed, Blair Spittal scoring twice to deny Hearts another win after a Liam Boyce strike and a sublime Kingsley free kick.

The month was rounded off with a comprehensive 3-0 win over Livingston: Michael Smith, Alex Cochrane, and, yes, you guessed it; Liam Boyce scoring to make it another win for the Hearts!

NOVEMBER

The Jambos responded emphatically to defeat in the Granite City, kicking off November with a 5-2 demolition job of Dundee United at Tynecastle. Ben Woodburn was superb, scoring twice whilst Alex Cochrane, Stephen Kingsley and Aaron McEneff added the extras.

A sub-par performance at Fir Park followed, Motherwell winning 2-0 as Taylor Moore saw red. Connor Shields and Ricki Lamie delivered the goals.

An up and down November was capped off on a high as Hearts put St. Mirren to the sword in Gorgie. A Gary Mackay-Steven strike coupled with another lovely free-kick from Kingsley sent the bruised Buddies back across the M8 with their tails between their legs.

DECEMBER

There was a real sense of injustice as December started; a 1-0 win for Celtic in Glasgow came through a Kyogo Furuhashi goal – with replays showing that the Japanese forward was offside.

Hearts followed up with a 1-0 win over Livingston in West Lothian before Rangers came to Tynecastle and scored twice to win. A run of two wins on the spin followed; Jamie Walker emerging from the Dens Park fog late on to see off Dundee, whilst Michael Smith and Ben Woodburn struck to sink the Staggies at Tynecastle.

The final match of 2021 was played behind closed doors, with Scotland's winter break brought forward as Scotland returned to harsher lockdown restrictions.

JANUARY

Fortunately, fans were back quickly as Scottish football returned from the break. Josh Ginnelly scored twice against St. Johnstone at Tynecastle to kick start the new year with a bang. Celtic were up next, and floored Hearts with two first-half goals at home to leave with all three points.

Hearts' January shopping had seen Nathaniel Atkinson and Toby Sibbick join Hearts, but it was

on-loan Everton striker Ellis Simms who made an explosive mark in Gorgie, scoring the second goal in a 2-0 win over Motherwell at Tynecastle.

The Jambos also made the fifth round of the Scottish Cup, sweeping aside Ayrshire junior side Auchinleck Talbot with a 5-0 win at Beechwood Park.

FEBRUARY

Into February and a slump in form. A 0-0 draw with Hibs in the derby at Easter Road was followed by a 5-0 defeat at Rangers, with the boys in maroon also slipping to a 2-1 defeat to Dundee at Tynecastle and another 2-1 defeat to St. Johnstone in Perth.

A gruelling 120th-minute penalty shoot-out win over Livingston in the Scottish Cup followed before an unpleasant month ended with an enjoyable win over St. Mirren in Paisley; Cammy Devlin scoring his first goal for the club whilst Ellis Simms bagged the other.

APRIL

April started with a 1-1 draw against Ross County in Dingwall, before Hearts wrapped up third place and European football with a derby demolition of Hibs! Andy Halliday scored twice to silence the noisy taunts from the Hibs fans in the Roseburn Stand. The following week, we did it again – this time at Hampden! Ellis Simms and Stephen Kingsley scored in a 2-1 win to dump our rivals out and send Hearts to the Scottish Cup final!

A depleted Hearts side then travelled up to Tayside for another Tannadice tumble, winning 3-2, before being held to a goalless draw at Tynecastle by Ross County.

MARCH

Hearts got their winning ways back up and running as spring sprung. We put in a dominant performance under the lights at Tynecastle to beat Aberdeen 2-0. A late Craig Halkett header earned the Jambos a point at Tannadice before heading back to Tynecastle to thump St. Mirren 4-2 in the quarter-final of the Scottish Cup – setting up a date with Hibs at Hampden!

The Jam Tarts then beat Livingston 2-0 – Beni Baningime scoring the first for Hearts before sadly suffering an injury that ended his season.

MAY

Into the final part of the season, as Hearts suffered three defeats on the spin. A 4-1 defeat at Celtic Park was first before losing 2-1 at Fir Park to Europe-chasing Motherwell. Rangers then won 3-1 at Tynecastle to bring the curtain down on the cinch Premiership season.

Up next was the Scottish Cup Final at Hampden. Rangers were the opponents once more. Despite a valiant effort in the 90 minutes, two extra time goals from Ryan Jack and Scott Wright were enough to see us off after a closely contested match.

And that was that; a remarkable first season for the boys in maroon back in the big time!

Snaps From a Season

David Mollison and James Christie are the club photographers at Hearts. They spent the 2021/22 season following HMFC up and down the country, home and away, as the boys in maroon enjoyed a very special season. Their pictures document Hearts' return to the Premiership, as we also enjoyed a season of full stands with life kicking off once again following the pandemic.

Neigh Funny Business

This Hearts fan enjoyed Craig Halkett's late equaliser at Ibrox! The big defender went up in the 89th minute to salvage a point for the Jam Tarts. Cue a great deal of horsin' around in the away end!

Kitted Out

A Hearts supporter takes in the view of our pre-season friendly against Sunderland. On a sun-kissed day at Tynecastle, it was only right that the must-have summer outfit for any Jambo was on display.

Jamie Didn't Mist

The Dundee defence holds its head in disbelief as Jamie Walker emerges from the fog with a later winner.

All Gone Quiet Over There

Hearts had plenty of reasons to keep opposition fans quiet over the course of the season, and here you can see Liam Boyce and Alex Cochrane issuing a polite reminder to some detractors.

Taking A Tumble

Hearts supporters take a tumble after wildly celebrating a goal in our Scottish Cup fourth round victory over Auchinleck Talbot. The Jambos won 5-0 with Andy Halliday, Peter Haring, Liam Boyce, and Alex Cochrane all getting on the scoresheet.

Yaaaaaasssss!

Cammy Devlin, that is all.

Did You Just See That?

Peter Haring and Andy Halliday watch on in disbelief as Barrie McKay scores a sensational first goal for Hearts against Livingston.

DERBY DELIGHT!

The 2021/22 campaign saw the Edinburgh derby reignited with Hearts and Hibs back together in the Premiership. It's the game that fans of both clubs look for when the SPFL release the fixture list for each season.

This campaign was a memorable one for Hearts. Two goalless draws in the first derbies of the season kept the bragging rights in the city on ice for a few months but when April rolled around; it was the boys in maroon who emerged as the capital's top club!

In a quirk of the scheduling, Hearts and Hibs had to face each other twice in the space of a week! The final league match before the split set up a derby at Tynecastle before the Scottish Cup pencilled the two sides in for a winner-takes-all showdown at Hampden Park in the semi-final of the competition.

If the normal pressure of a derby game wasn't enough, there was more than just pride at stake for Hearts. Victory at Tynecastle in the league match would guarantee that Hearts couldn't be caught in third place – whilst also guaranteeing a European play-off AND having the chance to crush Hibs' top six ambitions.

Meanwhile at Hampden, there's not much of an explanation required. Victory for either side in Glasgow would guarantee their place in the 2022 Scottish Cup Final. Oh, and a Hearts victory would mean that the Jambos would be one play-off win away from the Europa League group stages...

Hearts 3-1 Hibs: The Andy Halliderby!

Andy Halliday was the hero of the afternoon in Gorgie, scoring twice alongside a Stephen Kingsley piledriver to send Hibs tumbling into the bottom six.

The versatile Halliday is usually the hard-working cog in the midfield or deployed to patrol the flank on the left side. This time, Andy found himself bursting the net twice to silence a packed Roseburn Stand full of Hibs fans to write his name into derby folklore!

Hearts fans maybe didn't expect such a dreamy result, especially when there was a nightmare start. Drey Wright scored for Hibs after just five minutes, cutting inside and squeezing a shot into the net, aided by a slight nick off a Hearts shirt.

The afternoon appeared to be going their way as they continued to have the better of it in Gorgie, and they could have been further ahead. Wright had another effort deflected wide before Elias Melkersen twice found himself in possession in the box but could not get a shot away.

Hearts were reeling, but we found our feet and a flurry in front of goal brought two huge chances. A brilliant through ball from Barrie McKay sent Ellis Simms clear, but his lob over goalkeeper Matt Macey dropped the wrong side of the post.

Halliday was next with two wide shots, but when that third opportunity arrived, he made no mistake as Hearts levelled! Simms, despite being under huge pressure from the Hibs defence, slipped it into the path of Halliday, who applied a cool finish into the far corner.

Hearts carried that momentum straight into the second half and took a deserved lead on 47 minutes. After a corner failed to be cleared by the visitors, Peter Haring's superb cross was tapped in at the back post by Kingsley to send Tynecastle wild.

But that was nothing compared to the scenes just shy of the hour. McKay bamboozled the Hibs defence with a lovely back heel for Halliday who drove for goal and smashed a screamer in off the post from 25 yards!

Hearts 2-1 Hibs: Hampden heroes!

Hearts saw off Hibs to reach the 2022 Scottish Cup Final after a hard-fought win at Hampden Park!

Two absolute beauties from Ellis Simms and Stephen Kingsley had Hearts two goals up in 20 minutes but Chris Cadden equalised for Hibs shortly after.

Joe Newell saw red for Hibs in the second half, as the Jambos held onto their lead to secure European group stage football next season for the first time in 18 years.

There was an expected cagey start to affairs with neither team able to get a foothold on proceedings but a moment of magic opened the scoring.

Hibs had possession near halfway but Alex Cochrane did well to win the ball and feed Barrie McKay. He slid a ball through for Ellis Simms and the big striker fired an absolute rocket from 25 yards out that flew past Matt Macey.

The Hearts tails were up now, and a moment of sheer genius doubled the lead. Stephen Kingsley lined up a free kick from 30 yards out but instead passed to Liam Boyce who teed up Kingsley to bend a sensational left footed strike into the top corner.

It seemed like one way traffic but Hibs were back in the match almost immediately. Lewis Stevenson cut a ball back for Chris Cadden whose first shot was blocked, but the second with his left foot found the corner of the net. There was to be no further response from Hibs, and Hearts cruised to the finish line with the victory.

Two wins out of two in one week for the Jambos. Victory in the derby goes to Hearts. Again.

Forever Hearts
Player of the Year 2021/22

Legends of the past and the present were honoured at the EICC, as the great and the good of Heart of Midlothian gathered for the club's "Forever Hearts" ceremony.

Hosted by Scott Wilson, Player of the Year and the Hall of Fame were merged into one memorable evening as fans raised a toast to Robbie Neilson and his squad as they marked a successful campaign on the park that saw third place, a cup final spot, and European football sewn up in style.

Jim Brown, Bobby Kirk and the 2012 Scottish Cup winning team were inducted to the Hall of Fame as the club sealed their names forever in our triumphant history, with scarcely a dry eye in the house as we paid an emotional tribute to the dearly missed Marius Žaliūkas. It was a successful night for Craig Gordon and Stephen Kingsley, whilst members of the Hearts Women squad were also honoured for the first time in the club's history. The winners were as follows:

Fans and Players' Player of the Year: Craig Gordon

What a season it was for our hometown hero. The skipper's world class performance between the posts was recognised by supporters and his teammates on the same weekend he made his 250th appearance for the club against Celtic at Parkhead.

Craig cleaned up and scooped both gongs. Our captain spoke at length about what Hearts means to him and how proud he was to be recognised by the fans and his fellow players.

Goal of the Season: Stephen Kingsley v Hibs

With so many memorable maroon strikes in season 2021/22, Hearts supporters had a job on their hands selecting a winner.

Stephen Kingsley's iconic free kick against Hibs at Hampden came out on top, with a boisterous roar going up in the room as replays of his goal were played on the big screen.

Hearts Women Player of the Year & Rising Star: Georgia Hunter and Lisa Rodgers

On their bow at the club's award ceremony – teenage goalkeeper Lisa Rodgers took home the Dell Technology Rising Star prize for her exceptional maturity between the sticks, whilst defender Georgia Hunter's composed displays at the back saw her secure the Pawprint overall Player of the Year. The duo were presented with their prizes by Eva Olid.

Wallace Mercer Special Recognition: Clare Cowan

In 2006, the club decided to put up a new award for someone who had left a significant imprint on the club. This inaugural award was presented to the late Wallace Mercer and honours an individual whose contribution to the club has been truly outstanding.

Clare is Head of Football Operations and one of the longest serving employees at the club, with over 25+ years of service at Tynecastle.

She's been a trusted confidant to generations of players and managers that have come through the doors at Hearts, always going above and beyond in her role to help.

The award was kept under wraps, with Clare surprised on the night. She was presented with her trophy by the family of the late, great Wallace Mercer.

Academy Player of the Season: James Wilson

James Wilson was recognised for his performances at the Hearts Football Academy with the overall Academy award. Young James has played and trained with the Under-18s this season, regularly featuring for Steven Naismith's young guns – including an impressive cameo from the bench in the Youth Cup final against Rangers at Hampden. James spoke with a maturity beyond his years on stage and mentioned how seeing the likes of Makenzie Kirk and Murray Thomas make their senior debuts had him excited for the future at Hearts.

Meanwhile, the other winners were...

Doc Melvin Award - Garry Halliday

Hall of Fame - 2012 team, Jim Brown, Bobby Kirk, Marius Žaliūkas

2022/23
First Team Squad

Away up in Gorgie, at Tynecastle Park, there's a wee football team that'll aye make its mark... Get to know the players pulling on the famous maroon this season!

1

CRAIG GORDON

Position: Goalkeeper

Country: Scotland

Joined Hearts: 2020, second spell, from Celtic

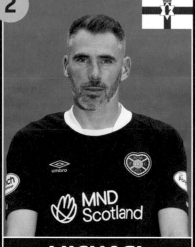

2

MICHAEL SMITH

Position: Defender

Country: Northern Ireland

Joined Hearts: 2017, from Peterborough United

3

STEPHEN KINGSLEY

Position: Defender

Country: Scotland

Joined Hearts: 2020, from Hull City

4

CRAIG HALKETT

Position: Defender

Country: Scotland

Joined Hearts:
2019, from Livingston FC

5

PETER HARING

Position: Midfielder

Country: Austria

Joined Hearts:
2018, from SV Ried

6

BENI BANINGIME

Position: Midfielder

Country: DR Congo

Joined Hearts:
2021, from Everton

7

JORGE GRANT

Position: Midfielder

Country: England

Joined Hearts: 2022, from Peterborough United

9

LAWRENCE SHANKLAND

Position: Striker

Country: Scotland

Joined Hearts:
2022, from Beerschot

10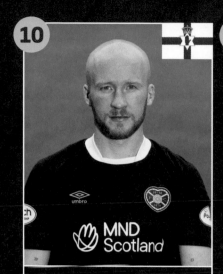

LIAM BOYCE

Position: Striker

Country: Northern Ireland

Joined Hearts:
2020, from Burton Albion

11

GARY MACKAY-STEVEN

Position: Forward

Country: Scotland

Joined Hearts:
2020, from New York City FC

12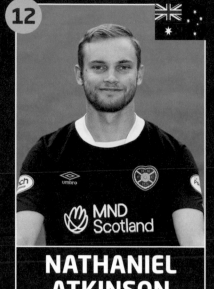

NATHANIEL ATKINSON

Position: Defender

Country: Australia

Joined Hearts:
2022, from Melbourne City

13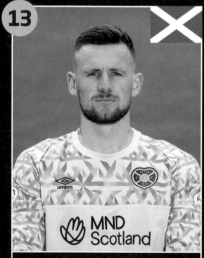

ROSS STEWART

Position: Goalkeeper

Country: Scotland

Joined Hearts:
2021, from Livingston FC

14

CAMMY DEVLIN

Position: Midfielder

Country: Australia

Joined Hearts:
2021, from Newcastle Jets FC

15

KYE ROWLES

Position: Defender

Country: Australia

Joined Hearts: 2022, from Central Coast Mariners

16

ANDY HALLIDAY

Position: Utility

Country: Scotland

Joined Hearts: 2020, from Rangers FC

17

ALAN FORREST

Position: Midfielder

Country: Scotland

Joined Hearts: 2022, from Livingston FC

18

BARRIE MCKAY

Position: Forward

Country: Scotland

Joined Hearts: 2021, from Swansea City FC

19

ALEX COCHRANE

Position: Defender

Country: England

Joined Hearts: 2022, second spell, from Brighton & Hove Albion

20

LEWIS NEILSON

Position: Defender

Country: Scotland

Joined Hearts:
2022, from Dundee United

21

TOBY SIBBICK

Position: Defender

Country: England

Joined Hearts:
2022, from Barnsley

22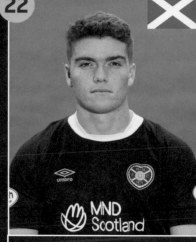

EUAN HENDERSON

Position: Striker

Country: Scotland

Joined Hearts:
Youth Academy Graduate

23

HARRY STONE

Position: Goalkeeper

Country: Scotland

Joined Hearts:
Youth Academy Graduate

24

SCOTT MCGILL

Position: Midfielder

Country: Scotland

Joined Hearts:
Youth Academy Graduate

25

CAMMY LOGAN

Position: Defender

Country: Scotland

Joined Hearts:
Youth Academy Graduate

27

CONNOR SMITH

Position: Midfielder

Country: Scotland

Joined Hearts:
Youth Academy Graduate

30

JOSH GINNELLY

Position: Forward

Country: England

Joined Hearts:
2021, from Preston North End

39

FINLAY POLLOCK

Position: Midfielder

Country: Scotland

Joined Hearts:
Youth Academy Graduate

WORDSEARCH

Find the Hearts related words in the grid. Words can go horizontally, vertically and diagonally.

K	J	E	P	S	Q	X	U	P	N	V	O	C	F	J	C
Q	V	J	H	Q	W	L	D	M	E	C	C	K	T	H	A
D	F	H	A	F	X	R	V	A	I	Q	Q	I	Y	Y	S
R	E	M	Q	Y	W	Y	Z	U	L	C	V	Y	N	L	T
M	A	B	P	L	U	C	X	L	S	R	X	P	I	C	L
H	A	S	D	Z	P	R	E	D	O	N	Y	A	E	A	E
B	R	R	I	A	L	N	N	L	N	V	O	Q	T	P	J
W	V	S	O	E	P	F	J	T	D	A	H	A	R	I	X
Y	G	N	M	O	G	O	R	G	I	E	U	D	O	T	P
D	P	E	Z	Y	N	D	Z	W	H	K	C	M	C	A	Y
F	X	H	C	Z	V	K	Z	T	U	E	H	C	K	L	F
R	Y	J	J	Q	M	D	M	C	K	A	Y	J	G	L	U

McKay   **Dalry**

Tynie   **Gorgie**

Auld   **Neilson**

Castle   **Capital**

Rock   **Maroon**

ANSWERS ON PAGES 60-61

SPOT THE BALL

Can you spot which is the real ball in the photos below?

ANSWERS ON PAGES 60-61

GUESS THE PLAYER!

Can you guess which former Hearts player I am based on the clues below?

1: I scored 27 derby goals against Hibs

2: I played for Newcastle United before returning to Hearts for a second spell

3: I have also been manager of Hearts

4: I was also manager at Inverness Caledonian Thistle

5: I retired in 2000

The answer is:

ANSWER ON PAGES 60-61

THE BIG HEARTS Quiz of 2023

Fancy yourself as a know-it-all about the boys in maroon? Think you know your Hearts history? Know the difference between Rudi and Robbo? See if you can get all the right answers in the quiz below.

1: Who scored our first goal in our first game back in the Premiership when we beat Celtic 2-1 at Tynecastle on the opening day?

2: I'm a forward who signed for Hearts in 2021, and have previously played for Rangers, Nottingham Forest, and Swansea City. Who am I?

3: I scored the first goal in our 2022 Scottish Cup semi-final win over Hibs. Who am I?

4: Which famous football stadium architect designed the old Main Stand at Tynecastle? He also designed Anfield, Celtic Park, and Old Trafford.

5: How many clean sheets did Craig Gordon keep in the 2021/22 season?

6: Who was Hearts' top goal scorer last season with sixteen goals?

7: Which Hearts player made his 250th appearance for the club at Celtic Park on the 7th May 2022?

8: Which Hearts player scored two goals against Hibs at Tynecastle on the 9th April 2022 to put the Easter Road team into the bottom six?

9: I have won two Scottish Cups with Hearts, in 2006 and 2012. I scored in both finals. Who am I?

10: Who was Hearts manager when we won the league title in 1960?

ANSWERS ON PAGES 60-61

33

HEARTS WOMEN
The Gorgie girls are on the up!

There's a sense of new beginnings around women's football in Scotland, and Eva Olid is focused on building up that sense of optimism as Hearts Women upgrade to semi-professional status.

With elite women's football set to come under the control of the SPFL from next season, the move represents another critical evolution at the club – moving with the times to reflect the upcoming merger with the professional game and improve standards of football, whilst bridging the gap with more established teams in the league.

Since taking the reigns at Hearts back in the summer of 2021, Eva has focused on developing the players as well as implementing a professional training regime alongside the dedicated sports science department and nutritionist at Oriam.

Following enthusiastic conversations with Joe Savage and the board; the move to semi-professionalism aims to attract new players with fresh investment, the chance to use world-class training facilities at Oriam, and the prospect of being involved on big stages – as seen when Tynecastle hosted the recent Edinburgh derby.

Having secured an initially small group of first-team players on contracts until 2023, and with more changes set to take effect over the coming months, Eva says she's driven and energised as standards are enhanced on and off the park.

"The merger with the SPFL gives us possibility and the aspirational goal of having a professional future for Hearts Women," she said.

"Our aim is having professional players, focused entirely on competition instead of working jobs or studying.

"My vision for the women's game in Scotland is that we reach a stage where every team is in the same position under a professional league. This will make the game more competitive and balanced, and the differences will not be as big as they are now with the gaps in resources.

"Since I have arrived here, I have seen the difference increased training has made to the team. They couldn't create many opportunities to score but we have now seen a big change in attack and their style of play with the ball. Our next task is to find that balance, but I am confident that we will make the adjustments and our future will be very bright."

The change in status has the full backing of the club's Board of Directors and is rooted in raising standards. It's a vision that's fully supported by Joe Savage, with our Sporting Director helping oversee the upgrade as it takes off in the initial stages.

Joe is excited by the fresh canvas to work with and believes there's even more to come from Eva Olid and Hearts Women as the club takes its first steps on a new journey.

"We absolutely needed further professionalisation for the women's team. They've been working on a voluntary basis for a long time, so if we wanted to take the next step as a club and attract a better calibre of footballer – we need to start paying players," he explained.

"The club created a budget for this year, and we're going to be adding more to that for next season. Eva and her staff have done a really good job so far, and we think there's more to come because of how she operates and develops players.

"The squad now comprises of young ladies, and this year will be a great learning curve for them and an experience, but we also want to be as competitive as we can."

Exciting times for women's football and Hearts Women. The future is bright, the future is maroon!

YOUNG HEARTS RUN FREE
ONES TO WATCH

This season has seen nine of Hearts' brightest academy talents put pen to paper on their first professional contracts at Tynecastle Park, whilst several of our academy graduates have even got the chance to play for the senior side!

Under the watchful eye of Academy Director Frankie McAvoy, these Wee Jambos will be hoping to make their mark as they push for a spot in the Hearts first team. Frankie said, "I'm absolutely delighted that a number of our players have been given a chance to step into the full-time environment. Hopefully within that environment they can flourish and become proven players.

"Our aim, hopefully, is to get them ready for Robbie's first team. Boys like Murray Thomas and Makenzie Kirk got a chance in the latter part of last season which was great to see. Now this group have a chance to push forward and thrive."

Be sure to keep an eye on these young prospects...

MAKENZIE KIRK
NORTHERN IRELAND FORWARD

A clever and live wire attacker, Makenzie Kirk is one of the finest finishers at the academy.

The son of former Hearts striker Andy Kirk, Makenzie has followed in the footsteps of his father at both club and country – having made his debut for both the first team at Tynecastle and the Northern Ireland Under-19s.

Makenzie played for Northern Ireland at the Football Federations Cup in Spain in early 2022.

MURRAY THOMAS
SCOTLAND FORWARD

A young man who has made a big impact since arriving at Hearts in November 2021, attacker Murray has been a frequent scorer in the Under-18s for Steven Naismith's team. A big strong player, with great close control on the ball, a player who is developing really well.

Scored in last season's Youth Cup final against Rangers.

ADAM FORRESTER
SCOTLAND
CENTRE BACK

Adam came in from Rangers in November 2021 and has slotted in well into life at the Hearts Football Academy at Riccarton. Technically gifted, right footed but able to play on the right and left side.

Steps out and reads the game well with a good change of pace. Integral member of the Under-18s squad that made last season's Youth Cup Final.

BOBBY McLUCKIE
SCOTLAND
LEFT BACK /
LEFT WING BACK

LIAM McFARLANE
SCOTLAND
GOALKEEPER

A cracking prospect that has been with the club for a number of years. Joined the academy in 2017 from Penicuik and is a member of Hearts' Balerno performance school programme.

A great talent on the ball, left footed, lots of energy to get up and down the park. Another player who was a key figure in our run to the 2022 Youth Cup final.

A towering young goalkeeper, Liam has made a number of impressive saves in his time at the Hearts Football Academy.

Regular followers of the Wee Jambos will know about his consistent excellence in the league, but Liam caught national attention after a sterling performance in the Youth Cup final that kept Rangers at bay.

A calming presence at the back, with incredibly keen reflexes to pull off stretching saves. Had a brief spell on loan at Montrose last season.

A Tribute to Alan Anderson

By David Speed

We sadly bid farewell to a Hearts legend this year, saying goodbye to our former captain Alan Anderson - one of the greatest to ever wear maroon.

A part of being a Hearts supporter is learning about the people that helped make us great. Club historian David Speed provides an insight into what our legendary former skipper was like:

"On and off the field, he represented Hearts with distinction and when Alan was inducted into the Hall of Fame in 2018, the emotion in the Gorgie Suite was tangible.

Born in Edinburgh on 21 December 1939, Alan was a lifelong Hearts supporter who was immensely proud to eventually captain the club over many years.

As a youngster, the steadfast defender represented Leith Primary Schools and after moving up to David Kilpatrick's Secondary, he played for Edinburgh in the Scottish Schools' Cup. Alan also progressed his game with United Crossroads Boys Club and the muscular centre-half briefly appeared for Dalkeith Thistle Juniors before joining Falkirk in June 1958.

He also had a short spell on loan to Alloa Athletic before transferring to Millwall in September 1959. While in London, Alan finished his apprenticeship as a compositor and in 1961/62, he assisted Millwall to win the Fourth Division Championship.

In July 1962, a £10,000 fee took the rugged centre-half to Scunthorpe United, but he never settled in the town and in November 1963, at the age of 23, Alan came to Hearts for £1,500. This was surely one of the club's greatest-ever bargains, because the 6'1" defender became one of Hearts' most admired players, being a formidable obstacle for opponents and particularly strong in the air.

He was also a wonderful servant, playing a remarkable 537 times for Hearts (of which 475 were competitive games). In addition to commanding the rearguard, Alan always had presence at set pieces and he scored a creditable 37 goals (31 in competitive matches).

Regretfully, like so many of our fine players, he was always a runner-up, appearing in the 1968 Scottish Cup Final against Dunfermline Athletic; the 1971 Texaco Cup Final against Wolverhampton Wanderers; and being a member of the squad that lost the League Championship on goal average in 1964/65.

Nevertheless, he proudly represented the club in the summer of 1964 at the New York Soccer League and later prestigious tours of Ireland, the USA, Norway and the Netherlands. The inspiring stopper saw European action in 1965/66 and also represented Scotland seven times on the SFA World Tour in 1967.

Alan Anderson
Forever in our Hearts
1939-2022

Alan assisted Hearts into the initial Premier Division (1975/76) and to also reach the Scottish Cup Final that season, although he missed the Hampden match. Alan then retired in May 1976 to pursue a successful career as a publican, sports shop proprietor and hotelier. He was also a fine golfer.

He might have been brought up in the streets of Leith, a short distance from Hibernian's ground, but his heart was always maroon. The heartfelt sympathy of everyone connected with Heart of Midlothian is extended to his wife, Annette, and his family for their great loss.

Alan Anderson was a Hearts man through-and-through and was proud to make over 500 appearances and captain the team that he loved."

Scott Wilson
A Life on the Tannoy

We marked the end of an era last season as Scott Wilson, 'The Voice of Tynecastle' stepped down after nearly 20 years as the club's iconic stadium announcer.

Fans of a certain age will never have known Tynecastle without Scott. He's been a constant presence in Gorgie for the best part of two decades, narrating unforgettable matches, moments and goals. His instantly recognisable voice was part of the matchday fabric at Tynecastle.

On the 30th April 2022, after a 0-0 draw with Ross County in Gorgie, he put the stadium microphone down for the very last time. Club captain Craig Gordon ran into the stand and brough Scott onto the pitch as Tynecastle rose to applaud a proper Hearts man.

Although he's not quite riding off into the sunset yet (he'll continue to host the Gorgie Suite matchday hospitality next season), it was nonetheless a significant moment in Hearts history.

Scott first made his mark in Gorgie on 10th August 2002.

"Jambos everywhere remember the day fondly – albeit not because of me! You see, I happened to make my first appearance as stadium announcer alongside another debutant: Mark de Vries!", Scott explains.

"He scored four goals in a 5-1 win over Hibs that day. I remember preparing for the match and cutting up five songs to use as goal celebrations thinking they'd do me for the four or five matches I intended to host. I ended up having to use them all in the first game!

"Before Hearts, I was the play-caller for the Scottish Claymores, an American football team. Chris Robinson, the Hearts chief at the time, was at one game looking for inspiration because his intention was to the change the matchday experience at Hearts.

"I said I'd host five or so games whilst Hearts trained up a new announcer; we lost only one of those first five and I never left."

LET'S MAKE

From team line ups to safety messages, goal announcements and substitutions, Scott is the voice of authority at Tynecastle, but if there's one thing we'll miss the most, it's that iconic catchphrase.

"The 'Let's Make Some Noise' catchphrase is actually something I've used ever since I started hosting live sports events. I've hosted American football, baseball, rugby, basketball, ice hockey and of course, football. I've used it at every event. Of course, the full length "This Is Tynecastle" version debuted on 10th August 2002 and has remained in place ever since," he explains.

It's important to remember that Scott is a Jambo like the rest of us. So what's it like to have to instantly compose yourself after a goal?

"The hardest part of the job is remembering to be a professional before being a fan as it's very easy to get carried away when we're playing well and when we score. I still smile when people send me the YouTube footage of Osman Sow's injury-time goal against Celtic when I was announcing the time added on and I lost it... just a wee bit!

"Sometimes it's difficult to bite your lip when the referee, in my opinion, has made a mistake and, in my opinion, they seem to make many!

"The most rewarding part is having the best seat in the house and to be sat next to my son Chris who plays the music. It's also amazing, as a fan, to be able to interview Hearts players past and present on the field and in our suites, and to become pally with them.

"I'm just a fan that was lucky enough to get an incredible chance to become the voice of Tynecastle and I hope that I've done the club proud. I'd like to think that, for the most part, I've been professional and haven't noised the visiting fans up too much!

"I've been lucky to meet many footballers and celebrities during my career and those that stand out for being a great personality is Jose Quitongo. He's not only the coolest dude I know, he's also fantastic to interview. He never takes himself seriously and is a great laugh."

Most Hearts fans will argue it's us Jambos that have been lucky to have Scott on the mic for so many years. So why has he now decided to call it a day?

"I'm a great believer that all good things must come to an end. I was keen to relinquish this role on my terms and when I was still competent at it.

"My 20th anniversary seemed like as good a time as any to make that move. Of course, I'll miss the role but I'll still be at every home match. Some of the players we've signed really excite me and makes me think we're at the start of something really great here at Tynecastle.

"It's a fantastic time to be a Hearts fan and a co-owner of the club that my family and I have supported all of our lives. Let's continue to get behind them. This is Tynecastle, let's make some noise!"

SOME NOISE!

Centenary of the Heart of Midlothian War Memorial at Haymarket

April 9th 2022 marked 100 years since the Heart of Midlothian War Memorial was erected at Haymarket. The site of this memorial has seen major changes through the years, but one constant remains; the annual Remembrance Sunday gathering as supporters, players and staff reflect in honour of all those caught in conflict around the world, past and present.

ARMISTICE

On 11th November 1918, the Armistice brought the Great War to an end. The enormous scale of casualties, with 700,000 killed and more than twice that number wounded, meant that every family and community in the United Kingdom was affected. Those who died in service overseas could not be brought home, and indeed, many of those who perished were never found.

As a consequence, there was a need for families, friends and communities to commemorate those who were lost and war memorials were raised around the country. At that time, the directors of Heart of Midlothian were humbled by the esteem in which

the club was held and the overwhelming demand for a memorial to its players and members who died in the Great War. Accordingly, Hearts vowed to erect a fitting memorial and in August 1919, the Chairman, Elias Furst, formed a committee to make it happen.

THE HEART OF MIDLOTHIAN WAR MEMORIAL

A traditional stone memorial was considered a fitting tribute and Edinburgh Corporation authorised a site on the major junction at the foot of Ardmillan Terrace. By the end of January 1922, the memorial was complete, taking the form of a stone column surmounted with two pedimented clock faces.

The names of the leading battles of the Great War were carved on the column and a plaque was added stating: 'Erected by The Heart of Midlothian Football Club to the memory of their players and members who fell in the Great War 1914-19'. It was created by the renowned sculptor, Mr Henry Snell Gamley from a design by Sir Duncan Rhind, and was built by John Angus & Sons whose works were in Duff Street, near Tynecastle.

Shortly after completion there was an unexpected setback when Edinburgh Corporation required the proposed site of the memorial for new tram links linking Ardmillan Terrace to Dalry Road. Nevertheless, the Corporation saved the day through offering a splendid alternative at the horses' trough outside Haymarket Station.

THE UNVEILING

The War Memorial was unveiled on Sunday 9th April 1922. The scene was one of the most remarkable ever witnessed in the city, with an immense crowd of around 35,000 gathered at Haymarket and the surrounding streets. The band of the Highland Light Infantry (the 71st Highlanders) played sacred music for an hour before the ceremony and then at three o'clock, the vast audience watched the very moving unveiling of the Memorial by the Right Hon. Robert Munro, MP, the Secretary of State for Scotland.

Emotions ran high when the Secretary of State reminded the crowd, "Some of these lads fell in the Battle of the Somme. They fell in the morning of their days, with the dew of health upon their brows."

Hearts' Chairman, Elias Furst, had been ill and watched from a neighbouring window and so the club's Senior Director, William Burns, handed over

custody of the memorial to the Rt. Hon. the Lord Provost Thomas Hutchinson. The Lord Provost said that it would be preserved with all reverence for all time. Flowers were then laid by the many friends of the club from the world of football, politics and the military.

THE FUTURE

Today, Haymarket is an up-and-coming area of Edinburgh, increasingly modern, but enhanced by several sites of historical significance. This includes the Hearts' War Memorial and the Annual Remembrance Service, the value of which is clearly shown by the wonderful attendance that regularly reaches 1,500 in all weather conditions.

To mark the centenary, the club – in partnership with McCrae's Battalion Trust and the Foundation of Hearts – is set to refurbish the clocktower and surrounding island area, with the work scheduled for completion in November 2022.

We continue to remember the greatest, who gave it all.

Around the continent with Hearts:
OUR EURO TRIPS

As Heart of Midlothian gear up for our return to European football for the first time in six years, it's only right we remember some memorable trips around Europe of years gone by! From Anfield to Amsterdam, the boys in maroon have tested themselves against some steely opposition when we've travelled overseas. Take a look at the postcards below to see where we've been around Europe...

2012: LIVERPOOL 1-1 HEARTS, ANFIELD, ENGLAND

Long before Jürgen Klopp steered them to Premier League and Champions League glory, Brendan Rodgers' Reds squared off against the Jam Tarts at Anfield - one of football's cathedrals.

The Europa League play-off round had thrown Hearts and Liverpool together for a two-legged tie. In the first match in Gorgie, the two sides had both gone close for goals, but it was the English giants who would take a slender 1-0 lead back to Merseyside after Andy Webster scored an unfortunate own goal for Hearts.

A large travelling support made the short journey from Edinburgh to the north-west of England with little expectation. Rodgers, sensing the need for Liverpool to secure a better result after their struggle at Tynecastle, restored key players such as Steven Gerrard and Luis Suárez to the side.

Liverpool flew out the traps, but Hearts maintained a heroic defensive stand. With just five minutes left on the clock, David Templeton's shot squirmed through the gloves of Reds goalkeeper Pepe Reina - sparking delirious celebrations among Hearts fans.

Luis Suárez's killer instinct shone through to secure Liverpool a late equaliser, sending them through on aggregate. Still, a proud night to be a Jambo.

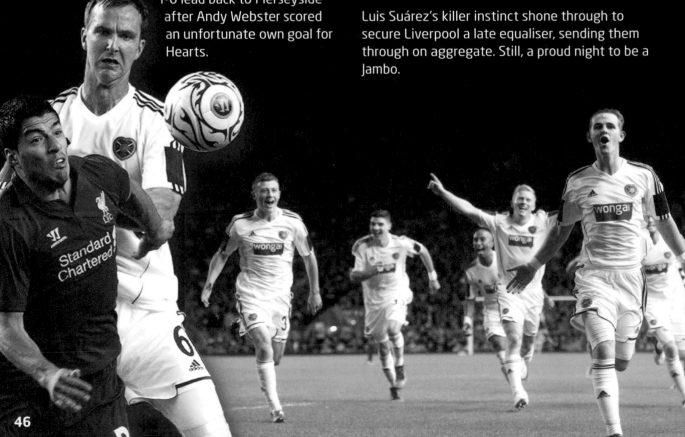

2003: BORDEAUX 0-1 HEARTS, STADE CHABAN DELMAS, FRANCE

Hearts boss Craig Levein took his team to the south of France to face stern opposition in Ligue 1 outfit Bordeaux in round two of the UEFA Cup. A gutsy defensive display saw the Gorgie boys escape with a narrow first leg advantage.

Using a unique 6-3-1 formation in spells, the Jambos were forced to ride their luck on occasion as the hosts, featuring experienced international players such as Jean-Claude Darcheville, Mauricio Pochettino and a young Merouane Chamakh, piled on the pressure.

As was so often the case for Hearts in Europe, the big moment came late on. Kevin McKenna cracked the bar from Paul Hartley's free-kick. The ball quickly bounced back into play and Hearts striker Mark De Vries was quickest to react, steering the ball in to pick up an impressive win against the Frenchmen.

2004: FC BASEL 1-2 HEARTS, ST. JAKOB-PARK, SWITZERLAND

A young defender called Robbie Neilson scored his first goal for Hearts in this electric European away tie in Switzerland. The Jambos found themselves in Group A of the UEFA Cup when they headed to St. Jakob needing points to keep the European dream alive.

Ramón Pereira set up Dennis Wyness for the opening goal, giving Hearts a perfect start to proceedings after half an hour. Argentine substitute César Carignano produced a clever chip over the keeper to give Basel an equaliser, but Robbie drove the winner home into the far corner in the dying minutes to earn a significant win. We wonder what Robbie Neilson is doing now?

2004: BRAGA 2-2 HEARTS, ESTÁDIO MUNICIPAL DE BRAGA, PORTUGAL

Hearts reached the group stage of the UEFA Cup in thrilling fashion, knocking out Portuguese side Braga 5-3 on aggregate. Andy Webster, Paul Hartley and Patrick Kisnorbo scored for Hearts in a 3-1 win in the first leg at Murrayfield, knowing there was still a job to do in the second leg.

It looked like it might have been a nervous night in Portugal when João Tomás netted an early opener, but Mark De Vries was the man to turn things around either side of half-time, scoring twice. By this stage, the Portuguese needed four goals to progress. Hearts held on, and became the first-ever Scottish and British club to make the group stages of the UEFA Cup.

LOCAL LEGEND
Gary Locke

Gary Locke knows how important your reputation is in football.

He knew when he pulled on the famous maroon jersey for the first time in 1993. He knew when he was manager, as Hearts defiantly crushed Hibs' relegation dreams in 2014. He knows now, perhaps more keenly than ever, that he's the Principal Ambassador for Heart of Midlothian Football Club in 2022.

Over the course of two decades of service at Tynecastle, few men have better embodied what it means to be a Jambo than Lockie. His never-say-die attitude as a player, driven by a love for the club, has translated seamlessly into his current role enhancing the good name of Hearts both at home and abroad as a valued member of the commercial department.

This season, the club welcomed Stoke City to Edinburgh in a pre-season clash that doubled as Lockie's testimonial. The Jambos came out on top, with Lawrence Shankland scoring twice in a 2-1 win. It was a day of celebration, even if the man himself was unlikely to ever think along those lines.

"I certainly never expected it," he said. "I'd been here just short of ten years when I was a player, two months short exactly. When I left, I never thought it would happen. Then one day, the boss {Ann Budge} stopped me and said, 'Do you realise you've just hit twenty years with the club? We'd like to reward you for your service.'

"I'm over the moon. I can't thank the board enough for letting it happen. I'm glad people turned up and enjoyed the game. I didn't even see it as being about me - I was just looking forward to watching the boys prepare for the new season and catching up with a few ex-teammates who came along to support me on the day."

It's testament to the man that even after many years, his name still commands such respect. Pasquale Bruno and José Quitongo are just some of the storied names that returned to Gorgie to support their old friend and colleague.

With two decades of service under his belt, it's natural to remember where it all started. Gary Locke, a man of Bonnyrigg, had a far from certain start to life with his boyhood heroes. In fact, it wasn't always guaranteed he would sign for Hearts at all.

"You get a lot of people in life who say their dream is to play for Barcelona, Real Madrid, or Liverpool. My dream was to play for Hearts," he explained. "I followed them the length and breadth of the country, and in Europe as well.

"I was fortunate that when I was 15, I had an S-Form. I didn't sign it because I used to go down and train with Manchester United and a few other clubs. My Dad was a diehard Jambo and wanted me to sign for Hearts, but I liked having the chance to see other clubs.

"My heart eventually was set on playing for Hearts. It's funny because Hearts were probably one of the last clubs to ask me to train. I was delighted to come in; I got offered a two-year apprenticeship at the start of fourth year at school. From there, my mind was made up.

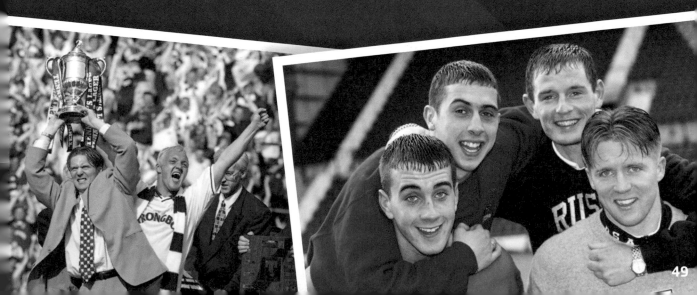

49

"I left school and went straight into Tynecastle; it was a dream come true."

There was still some work to do before he could stake his claim for a starting spot at Hearts. Any graduate of the academy soon found themselves undertaking a gruelling apprenticeship - led by a stern teacher in former Hearts striker Sandy Clark.

"I genuinely believe that the grounding I had at Hearts as a young player made me," says Gary. "I cleaned boots and changing rooms. Very few young lads that go into a club go on to make it as a professional.

"Sandy drummed that into us every day. If you didn't stick in at football, you might be doing this as a full-time job. I'm pretty sure most people would rather play in front of thousands of people every week rather than sweeping the streets.

"I made my debut on the Saturday, and then first thing Monday, I was back in at the stadium picking up litter from the terracing. I don't think it's a coincidence that a lot of the boys Sandy looked after went on to have good careers in the game, even if it wasn't always at Hearts."

It was no surprise that Lockie rose through the ranks quickly after that. His debut came against St. Johnstone at McDiarmid Park in May 1993, replacing Derek Ferguson after 43 minutes. He would quickly establish himself as a core figure within the team.

Jim Jefferies' arrival as manager at Tynecastle in 1995 was the beginning of a career-spanning partnership, with the new Hearts gaffer quickly installing the young Locke as club captain.

"You don't realise it at the time when you're playing. I got made Hearts captain when I was 20 years old," Gary smiles. "As a Jambo, I was obviously buzzing at what was a massive honour. It's not until you get older, and you look back, that you realise what an achievement it was."

How did his friends and family react, seeing their mate pull on the armband every week for the team they all grew up supporting?

"One moment stuck with me. I used to stand in the shed every week," he explained. "I remember one game against Hibs. I wasn't playing well; I was trying to kick everything apart from the ball. Later, I put in a good ball into Allan Johnston who got it down and scored.

"I ran to the shed to celebrate. It was surreal; I could see my brother, my dad, my mates. They're all going bananas because we got a late winner. I jumped on the fence, and they all got a hold of me. You knew you were living the dream when you remember that that was where I was standing as a fan all of six months ago. It took a wee while to sink in."

His tenure as skipper marked a historic time down Gorgie way. Jefferies started to assemble a side composed of blossoming Scottish talents like Colin Cameron and Steve Fulton, supplemented with fine foreign acquisitions in Stefano Salvatori and Giles Rousset.

For Lockie, it was a special time. "Hearts fans were great with me. I think they knew, especially when I was captain, that I wouldn't suffer fools," he said. "If a player wasn't trying or came to the club and were swanning about - I would be on them.

"That squad in 98, for me, were the pinnacle at Hearts. It was a group that were all desperate to win a trophy. Most of them became fans along the way. The dressing room was probably the best I've been involved in.

"They all wanted to work hard; not that the gaffer or Billy Brown would let them get away with it. They were sticklers for coming in every day, getting you to train how you played. If you didn't, they'd be on you.

"The dressing room was full of headbangers, but unbelievable players. We were quite lucky because we were mostly all the same age. We all hung about away from football. We would drink together. Go-karting. The boys would all go out for meals, they'd all be there, and the families would come as well. I think that spoke volumes.

"It was a laugh a minute. You look back now and can't help but smile - it was a very special time to be a Hearts player."

Lockie would leave Tynecastle in 2001, spending time at English first division side Bradford before enjoying a swansong in Ayrshire with Kilmarnock. A return to Hearts came in 2010 following his appointment as first-team coach under Jefferies in his second spell as manager.

"I'd been away for a few years, but I still followed the club. If I never had a game on a weekend, I would go and watch Hearts," he said.

"The one thing that disappointed me was that the name of the club was starting to become damaged. We weren't paying bills. It didn't sit right with me, the gaffer, or Billy. When you think of Heart of Midlothian; you think of McCrae's Battalion and the boys who went to war in the name of the club.

"Suddenly, you were speaking to people all around Edinburgh telling you about the state Hearts were in. It annoyed us. As much as clubs dislike each other on the pitch, Hearts' reputation had always been immaculate.

"Today, the name is what it should be. We pay bills. We don't mess anyone about."

Reputations - we know how important it is. These days, the club finds itself in much ruder health. There was no better man to fill the role of Ambassador when the job came up in 2017.

For a man who knows Hearts inside and out, there has scarcely been a better fit for the job.

"This right now is probably my dream position," said Gary. "You've got to carry yourself well and represent the club in the best possible way. The role's evolved in the five years since I came back but the fundamental part is that it's about making the club better in any way.

"If that's bringing in money, saying positive things. It's a big job. You want anyone associated with Hearts to carry the club in a good light. We've got that now. Even down to the people who sponsor us. It's all stuff I think the club should be doing. We want our younger fans to grow up and live their life right; we don't have any betting or vaping companies sponsoring us.

"Hopefully we can reflect that onto our fans. In their school, work, or daily lives. I know the history of the club, and I think I'm in a fortunate position. I'm not the daft 17-year-old from Bonnyrigg who joined Hearts all those years ago. I've got a lot of experience behind me now. I've seen a totally different side to the club in my current role which has a lot of responsibility.

"That's why we support Hearts. When the highs come along, they last for about two months. To see where we are now. To still be a part of it all, I couldn't be any happier."

Top row (left to right): Alex Cochrane, Josh Ginnelly, Scott McGill, Kye Rowles, Harry Stone, Ross Stewart, Nathaniel Atkinson, Andy Halliday, Gary Mackay-Steven, Michael Smith

Second row (left to right): Kit Manager Gordon Patterson, First Team Analyst Jake Sheard, Cammy Logan, Finlay Pollock, Craig Halkett, Peter Haring, Toby Sibbick, Lewis Neilson, Liam Boyce, Lawrence Shankland, Stephen Kingsley, Euan Henderson, Head of Performance Dr Bob McCunn, First Team Sports Scientist Mike Williams

Bottom row (left to right): First Team Physiotherapist
Craig Maitland, Cammy Devlin, Jorge Grant, Beni
Baningime, Lee McCulloch, Robbie Neilson, Craig Gordon,
Gordon Forrest, Paul Gallacher, Barrie McKay, Connor
Smith, Alan Forrest, First Team Physiotherapist Ross Grady

When Hearts Beat Bayern...

Bayern Munich... maybe you've heard of them? One of the biggest and most successful clubs in the world. Champions of Germany, European Cup winners, and home to some of the finest players on the planet. Did you know that we also beat them at Tynecastle once upon a time? No, we're not joking! This is the story of how the boys in maroon went toe-to-toe with one of Europe's elites and came out on top!

THE MATCH

Hearts: Smith, McKinlay, McPherson, McLaren, Levein, Berry, Galloway, Ferguson, Colquhoun, Black, Bannon

Bayern: Aumann, Grahammer, Pfluegler, Johnsen, Augenthaler, Flick, Koegl, Reture, Wohlfarth, Thon, Ekstrom

Bayern, managed by German football legend Franz Beckenbauer, touched down a chilly Edinburgh on a cold February morning. Much of the talk back in Germany wasn't worried if Bayern were going to take a commanding lead back to Munich, but rather that they already knew they would be!

Hearts, by contrast, had only been promoted back to the Scottish top-flight in 1983 –

slowly building themselves back up to one of the premier teams in Scotland under the guidance of Alex MacDonald and his assistant, Sandy Jardine.

To make matters more complicated, Hearts' legendary striker John Robertson was only fit enough to make the subs bench after recovering from injury. In what proved to be a tactical masterstroke for the Jambos, Iain Ferguson took his place in the attack – looking to replicate his goalscoring feats for Dundee United where he scored against Barcelona at the Nou Camp a few years prior.

The match started cagily, with the men in maroon keen not to concede ground to their German opponents too early. Hearts survived a penalty shout after 13 minutes; a misplaced pass from Ferguson was hoovered up by Thon, who threaded a superb pass across to Swedish striker Johnny Ekstrom. Jambos

THE BACKGROUND

The story starts back in 1988. Hearts, managed by Alex MacDonald, had finished 2nd in the Scottish Premier Division in 1987/88 campaign, sealing qualification for the old UEFA Cup. The possibility of glamorous European ties awaited! Few could have predicted though the incredible run Hearts enjoyed, advancing all the way to the quarterfinals after seeing off opposition from Ireland, Austria, and Bosnia.

Into the last eight, and it was time for Hearts to really face the big guns. The names were plucked out the hat, and a two-legged tie with German giants Bayern Munich was pencilled in for the beginning of 1989...

defender Craig Levein challenged Ekstrom in the box, with Bayern screaming for a spot kick - but Austrian referee Helmut Kohl waved away their appeals.

After a shaky start, Hearts grew in confidence and started getting in the face of their German counterparts. Eamonn Bannon whipped a dangerous cross across goal which Bayern keeper Aumann quickly punched to safety. Tosh McKinlay drilled the ball into the net, but the Gorgie celebrations were cut short when the linesman chopped it off for offside.

Tempers were starting to fray as the first half drew to a close. The Germans were evidently frustrated by the resistance shown by their Scottish foes – and events reached a fever pitch when Kenny Black put in a heavy tackle on Reuter, sparking a furious shoving match.

Hearts emerged for the second 45 with the bit between their teeth. Levein made our intentions clear from the off with a lovely long pass to Ferguson who teed up Bannon, his first time effort rattling off a Bayern shirt.

The 26,000 Jambos inside Tynecastle roared their approval, as Hearts turned up the intensity. Kenny Black was then

chopped down on the edge of the area at the old shed end of the stadium.

Mike Galloway and Iain Ferguson presided over the resulting free kick. Bayern scarcely had any time to plan their defence, before Galloway cleverly rolled the ball to Ferguson who dispatched a rocket of a strike high into the opposition's net!

Pandemonium ensued at Tynecastle, as all of Gorgie let out a collective roar of joy. Hearts knew their lead was still slender, and quickly tried to add a second, with Ferguson and Colquhoun going close. Bayern, still dangerous despite this wound, were lethal on the counter - storming up the park on the counter with frantic energy.

Things weren't going Bayern's way though, and when Dave McPherson scooped a shot over the bar ten minutes from time, Beckenbauer's boys could sense they were beat. The whistle finally came, and Hearts had secured one of the club's greatest European triumphs.

Sadly, the second leg was to be Hearts' undoing, with Bayern scoring two goals in Munich to snatch victory. Either way, it was a special night to be a Jambo.

GETTING SHIRTY WITH IT
THE 2022/23 LOOK

Check out the new Umbro home kit for the 2022/23 season, with MND Scotland once again taking pride of place on the front of the jersey – complete with their brand-new logo, the helping hand of support.

The club's innovative sponsorship deal with Dell Technologies carries on into 2022/23 and we are delighted to continue to support the work of MND Scotland as we enter an exciting season of both domestic and European football. The response to our MND Scotland sponsorship, from Hearts supporters and the wider community, has been nothing short of remarkable. To date, we have raised an incredible £85,000 for the charity and we can't wait to see what the next season brings as we continue to raise awareness for such a vital cause.

The new 2022/23 home jersey features the club's traditional dark maroon throughout, complemented by a white collar and cuffs. The new MND Scotland logo adorns the front of the shirt. As well as the woven club crest, the jersey also features a bespoke heart on the cuff and the back of the neck.

The stunning 2022/23 away jersey features a distinct polka dot look, as the club puts an exciting modern spin on the classic inverted colours of the Heart of Midlothian away kit.

The returning Umbro third kit features black and blue stripes in homage to the much-loved 1993/94 'Inter Milan-style' away kit. Featuring a 2-colour gold and woven crest and a bespoke 'Jam tart' neck sign-off, the design also pays a subtle tribute to our home, Tynecastle Park, with a tonal stadium graphic running through the black stripes.

The stunning jersey is complemented by black shorts with a blue side panel, as well as blue socks with a black cuff turnover with 'HEARTS' on the back of the sock.

Get your hands on the new tops online at heartsdirect.co.uk, or in person at the Tynecastle Park club store!

THIS IS OUR HEARTS

MND Scotland

22.23 HOME KIT
HEART OF MIDLOTHIAN FOOTBALL CLUB

umbro

Quiz Answers

Spot the Ball - Page 31

Wordsearch - Page 30

K	J	E	P	S	Q	X	U	P	N	V	O	C	F	J	C
Q	V	J	H	Q	W	L	D	M	E	C	C	K	T	H	A
D	F	H	A	F	X	R	V	A	I	Q	Q	I	Y	Y	S
R	E	M	Q	Y	W	Y	Z	U	L	C	V	Y	N	L	T
M	A	B	P	L	U	C	X	L	S	R	X	P	I	C	L
H	A	S	D	Z	P	R	E	D	O	N	Y	A	E	A	E
B	R	R	I	A	L	N	N	L	N	V	O	Q	T	P	J
W	V	S	O	E	P	F	J	T	D	A	H	A	R	I	X
Y	G	N	M	O	G	O	R	G	I	E	U	D	O	T	P
D	P	E	Z	Y	N	D	Z	W	H	K	C	M	C	A	Y
F	X	H	C	Z	V	K	Z	T	U	E	H	C	K	L	F
R	Y	J	J	Q	M	D	M	C	K	A	Y	J	G	L	U

The Big Hearts Quiz of 2023
Page 33

1: Gary Mackay-Steven

2: Barrie McKay

3: Ellis Simms

4: Archibald Leitch

5: 20

6: Liam Boyce

7: Craig Gordon

8: Andy Halliday

9: Rudi Skácel

10: Tommy Walker

Guess The Player!
Page 32

I'm John Robertson!

Jock the Jambo has gone missing in the Hearts crowd at Tynecastle! Can you help us find him in the sea of maroon?